STRANMILLS COLLEGE BELFAST

SN 0074002 0

KV-638-692

B·I·B·L·E WORLD

BIBLE WORLD FACTFINDER

Herod's Temple

Herod the Great began building
the temple in Jerusalem in 19 BC.
The main building was complete
by the time of Jesus.

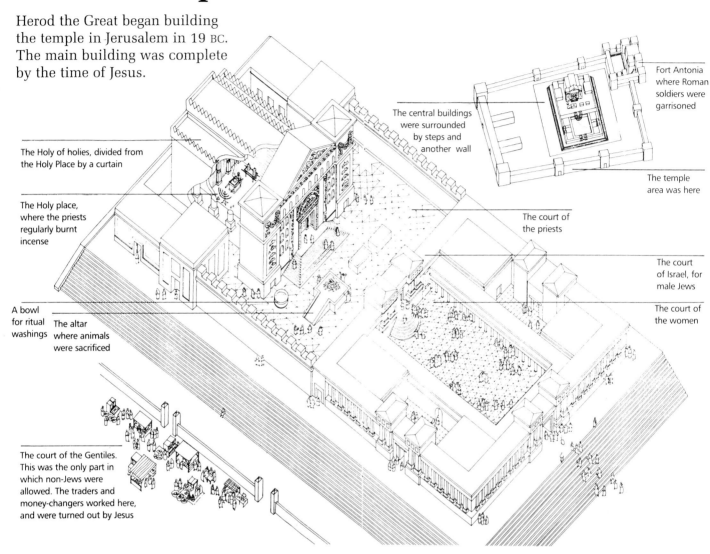

The Holy of holies, divided from
the Holy Place by a curtain

The Holy place,
where the priests
regularly burnt
incense

A bowl
for ritual
washings   The altar
where animals
were sacrificed

The court of the Gentiles.
This was the only part in
which non-Jews were
allowed. The traders and
money-changers worked here,
and were turned out by Jesus

The central buildings
were surrounded
by steps and
another wall

Fort Antonia
where Roman
soldiers were
garrisoned

The temple
area was here

The court of
the priests

The court
of Israel, for
male Jews

The court of
the women

This edition copyright © 1996 Lion Publishing

Published by
Lion Publishing plc
Sandy Lane West, Oxford, England
ISBN 0 7459 3202 9
Albatross Books Pty Ltd
PO Box 320, Sutherland, NSW 2232, Australia
ISBN 0 7324 1218 8

First edition 1996
10 9 8 7 6 5 4 3 2 1 0

All rights reserved

Acknowledgments
The illustrations in this book are copyright © 1991 and
1996 Lion Publishing.
Line drawings by Stanley Willcocks, Pauline O'Boyle,
Mark Astell, Dorothy Tucker, Vic Mitchell, Angela Pluess,
Simon Bull
Diagram by Tony Cantale
Time charts by Nicky Jex

A catalogue record for this book is available
from the British Library

Printed and bound in Malaysia

B·I·B·L·E W·O·R·L·D

BIBLE WORLD FACTFINDER

CONTENTS

A LION BOOK

A glossary of important words

Some of the explanations in this list have a word in *italic*. These words can also be looked up elsewhere in the glossary.

Altar
A place on which *sacrifices* were offered.

Angel
A messenger from God.

Apostle
Someone who is sent with a message. The first Christian apostles believed *God* had sent them to spread the message about Jesus.

Baptism
A ceremony of being washed in water as a sign of making a new beginning with *God*. Baptism had already been done before the time of Jesus, but it became the ceremony for marking a person's decision to follow Jesus.

Christ
A Greek word meaning 'anointed'... chosen to be a king. It is a title given to Jesus—'Jesus Christ'—by those who believed he was a special king sent by God. The Hebrew word 'Messiah' means the same thing.

Christian
A person who follows Jesus and believes that Jesus is the *Christ*.

Christianity
The *faith* of Christians.

Church
A group of Christians who meet to *worship* God together and to encourage one another in their *faith*.

Conversion
Being changed from one way of behaving to another. People who become Christians are sometimes called converts.

Covenant
An agreement or *testament*.

**Covenant box
(ark of the covenant)**
A special box made to hold *God*'s agreement with people, including God's *laws* (the *Ten Commandments*). It was kept in the *Holy of holies*. The covenant box has not been seen for hundreds of years, and was probably destroyed when the Babylonian army destroyed King Solomon's *temple* in Jerusalem.

Crucifixion
A Roman way of putting criminals to death by nailing them to a wooden cross. Jesus was put to death in this way.

Deacon
One who serves. Deacons in the early Christian *church* were people who helped organize everything the church wanted to get done.

Demons
Powers of evil.

Devil
The source of all evil.

Disciple
A learner or student, especially one who learned from a rabbi. Jesus' special followers were called disciples.

Exodus
The word means 'coming out'. In Bible history it usually refers to the time when Moses led the

▲ An Assyrian soldier taking captives into exile

Exile
Somewhere that is not your home where you are forced to live. In Bible history the word is mostly used to talk about the time the people of Judah were forced to leave their homes in and around Jerusalem and go and live in Babylon—the country of the enemies who had defeated them.

people of Israel on their escape from Egypt where they had been slaves. The story is told in the second book of the Bible, which is also called Exodus.

Gentile
Anyone who is not Jewish.

Holy Spirit
The invisible presence of *God*. Jesus' disciples received the Holy Spirit in a new way after his death and *resurrection*.

Festivals
Special times of celebration set aside to *worship God*. The main festivals of the people of *Israel* were set up in the time of Moses.

▶ The shofar – a ram's horn trumpet – was blown to announce the beginning of a festival.

Faith
Belief and trust in something that cannot be scientifically proved. Christians have faith that Jesus has accounted for all the wrongdoing of the world and made it possible for people to be *God*'s friends.

Forgiveness
Making peace between someone who has done wrong and the person who was hurt by that wrongdoing.

God
A being beyond this world and greater than it: a supreme being. Jews, Christians and Muslims believe that the God they worship made the world and everything in it.

Gospel
An account of the life of Jesus. The Bible has four Gospels, named after the people believed to have written them: Matthew, Mark, Luke and John.

This gave them the courage to begin telling everyone the news about Jesus.

Incarnation
Becoming a human being. In the Christian *faith* the belief that Jesus was *God* come to this world as a human being.

Incense
An expensive mixture of resins and spices that give off sweet-smelling smoke when they are burned. Israelite priests burned incense in the *tabernacle* and the *temple* to show how much they valued *God*'s presence. Incense smoke drifting up and away is also described in the Bible as a reminder of how people's prayers rise to God.

Holy of holies
The innermost part of the *tabernacle* and later the *temple*. The *covenant box*, containing God's laws—God's covenant with the people of Israel—was kept here. Only the high *priest* could enter the Holy of holies, and only on one day of the year (the Day of Atonement).

▶ The menorah – a golden lampstand with seven branches – stood in the *tabernacle* and later the *temple* just outside the Holy of holies.

Inspiration
How ideas come. Christians believe their Bible is inspired by *God*.

Israel

Israel was the name given to one of Abraham's grandsons. He was also called Jacob. His family grew and grew and became known as the people of Israel. Just after the time of King Solomon, the people of Israel quarrelled about the way the new king in Jerusalem was treating people. The people in the north set up a separate kingdom, called the kingdom of Israel. It was later destroyed by Assyrian enemies.

Jews

Descendants of the first people of Israel. Just after the time of King Solomon, the people of Israel quarrelled about the way the new king in Jerusalem was treating people. The kingdom split into two: *Israel* in the north and Judah in the south. Hundreds of years later, the people of Judah were beaten by Babylonian enemies and taken to live in exile in Babylon for about 40 years. Here, the people of Judah became known as Jews.

Kingdom (of heaven, of God)

Wherever God is recognized as being in charge. Christians believe that everyone who follows Jesus is part of *God*'s kingdom.

Last Supper

The special meal (probably a *Passover* meal) that Jesus had with his disciples, where he shared bread and wine with them and told them, when they did the same, to remember him. It was the beginning of the Christian ceremony of sharing bread and wine to remember Jesus' death. Christians today call the ceremony by different names such as the Mass, the Eucharist, Holy Communion and the Lord's Supper.

Levites

Assistant *priests*. They were in charge of music played in *God*'s *temple*.

Lord's Prayer

The special prayer Jesus taught his followers to say. It is sometimes called the 'Our Father', from the first two words of the prayer.

Messiah

The Hebrew word with the same meaning as *Christ*.

Law

Instruction about how to live. *God*'s laws in the Bible include both rules about what is right and wrong and stories that help people think it out for themselves.

▶ A *Jewish* man wears a box containing God's laws on his forehead – a reminder to keep them always in mind.

Miracle

A special event that cannot easily be explained. Why did something happen when it did? How did it happen? What does it mean? Jews and Christians see miracles as signs that *God* is at work.

Missionary

Someone who is sent out with a special job. Christian missionaries are set the job of spreading the news about Jesus. The *apostles* were missionaries.

Our Father

See *Lord's Prayer*

Passover

A meal the people of Israel ate just before Moses led them on the *Exodus* to freedom. They continued to celebrate Passover as a yearly festival to remember how God had helped them.

Pharisees

A religious group in the time of Jesus. Unlike the *Sadducees*, they tried to explain the old *law* of Moses to fit the situations they faced in their own times.

Pilgrim

A person who travels somewhere for a religious reason. The place they travel to is often an important centre for *worship*.

Prayer

Communicating with *God*. It includes talking and listening.

Parable
An everyday story with a deeper meaning. Jesus told parables: good stories about everyday things and people that helped people understand more about God.

Jesus' parables included stories about farming activities such as sowing (left) and reaping (right).

Priests
People specially chosen from the tribe of Levi to lead the people of *Israel* in *worshipping God* and helping them understand God's *laws*.

Prophet
A person with special wisdom sent by *God* with a message for people.

Psalms
A collection of poems to *God* in the Bible. They include hymns and prayers.

Rabbi
A teacher of *God's law* in the synagogue.

Resurrection
Jesus' coming to life again after his *crucifixion*.

Sabbath
The one day in seven set aside in *God's laws* as a day of rest.

Sacrifice
A special offering to a *god*.

Sadducees
A religious group in the time of Jesus. They believed only what was written in the first five books of the Bible—the books of Moses.

Salvation
Rescue. Christians believe Jesus brings salvation—rescues them from the consequences of *sin* by bringing *God's* forgiveness to people as *God incarnate*.

Sanhedrin
The Jewish religious council in the time of Jesus.

Saviour
One who brings *salvation*: a rescuer.

Scripture
The special writings of a religious *faith*. The Christian scriptures are the Bible: it includes the Hebrew Bible, which Christians call the Old Testament, and the writings of some of the first Christians, which they call the New Testament.

Septuagint
The name of a Greek translation of the *Jewish scriptures*, made well before the time of Jesus.

Sin
Wrongdoing; falling short of God's standards of what is right; turning away from God.

Synagogue
A meeting place. The *Jewish* people set up synagogues around the time Solomon's great *temple* in Jerusalem was destroyed and they had nowhere to meet to *worship God*. Soon there were synagogues in many countries of the ancient Near East. The rule for setting up a synagogue was that there must be at least 10 Jewish men to meet there.

Temple
A special place of worship. Solomon built the first temple to *God* in Jerusalem, on the hill sometimes called Mount Zion. It was destroyed by the Babylonians. A second temple was rebuilt by Zerubbabel. Just before the time of Jesus, the Jewish king Herod the Great

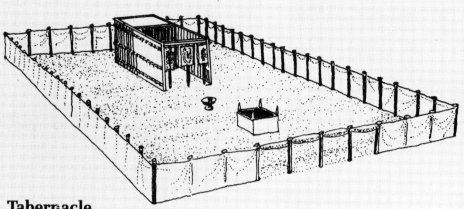

Tabernacle
A shelter or tent. The word is often used to mean the special tent the people of Israel built as a place to worship God when they were travelling from Egypt to Canaan in the time of Moses. The *covenant box* was kept in the *tabernacle* until the *temple* was built.

◀ This diagram shows the tabernacle in the process of being put up in a tent enclosure. Several layers of tent coverings still have to be laid over the tabernacle framework.

built a new temple. It was destroyed around 70CE by the Romans.

Ten Commandments
Ten great *laws* given to the people of *Israel* by God through their leader Moses. A copy of the Ten Commandments was kept in the *covenant box* in the place of worship—in the *Holy of holies* in the *tabernacle* and later the *temple*.

Testament
Another word for *covenant*, or agreement. Christians describe their Bible as having two main sections: the Old Testament, talking about the agreements God made with Noah, Abraham and Moses: and the New Testament, talking about the agreement Jesus arranged between God and people.

Trinity
A word used by Christians to describe how the one *God* can also be described as three:

God the Father, God the Son (Jesus) and God the *Holy Spirit*.

Worship
Giving praise and honour to a *god*, person or thing you consider to have great worth. For the people who worshipped the God of *Israel*, worship

included special ceremonies and *festivals*. The *prophets* also said that true worship meant living as God wanted and doing what was good and right and fair.

SPECIAL ASSIGNMENT

FILL IN THE BACKGROUND
One good idea for a project is to pick a story about a Bible character and then find out all you can about the way they lived. Say, for example, that you wanted to find out about Ruth (volume 2).

Where did she live? (Look up the page about Ruth in volume 2.)

What did the countryside around her look like? (Look up the place in volume 6.)

What period of Bible history did she live in?

What did people wear at that time? (Look up the pages about clothing in volume 8.)

What kind of house might they have had? (This is in volume 8 too.)

How did people worship God at that time?
Finding out the answers to these questions can make the story come alive in a new way.

Important Issues

What does the Bible have to say about the big questions of everyday life? Here are some of the starting points to help you find out.

Ambition

What is worth doing in life? The Bible stories say that people were made to love God and share in the work of looking after God's world (1/2). Jesus showed people how they could live as God's friends, and said that they could do this by following his example (4/14).

Bad things

The stories in the Bible say that the world has suffered bad things because people have turned away from God (1/2, 1/6, 10/10). Christians believe that Jesus came to beat all the powers of evil, and when he rose again from the dead he showed that death—the thing people fear most—is beaten (4/19). They believe that one day Jesus will bring in a new world, where there is no more pain or sadness (5/19, 10/20).

Children

The grown-up world sometimes treats children as unimportant. The Bible story of Samuel shows quite clearly that children are important to God (2/12 and 10/13). Jesus welcomed children and said they were very important in God's kingdom (4/8, 4/15).

Environment

According to the first stories in the Bible, God made a good and lovely world and cares for it (1/2, 1/5). God's good world was spoiled when people turned away from God (1/3). Jesus came to mend the relationship between God and the world: Christians believe that his calming a storm on Lake Galilee showed that this would include bringing calm and order into the whole world of nature (4/9).

Family life

The story of God's making the world shows that people were made to love and help one another (1/2, 1/3). When they turned away from God and acted selfishly, their relationships with each other were spoiled (1/3, 1/6). The rest of the Bible includes many stories of relationships that are a lot less than good... and some that are dreadful. Yet people who long to live as God wants can always find forgiveness and a new start. Examples to read about include Abraham (1/8), Jacob (1/10) and the woman caught having an affair whom Jesus was willing to forgive (4/15). The Bible's stories are written to show the belief that it is by putting God first that people's relationships with one another can begin to work.

Foreigners

The overall message of the Bible is that all people are important to God. God's laws told the people of Israel to treat foreigners well (2/11). The story of Jonah tells of God forgiving a foreign nation their wickedness (3/19). Foreigners are described as being among the first to see that Jesus was special (4/5). Jesus' story of the kind stranger reminded people that being God's people was more to do with how you lived than what nation you belonged to. The first Christians soon came to see that the good news of Jesus mending the friendship between God and people was for everyone (5/5) and all must learn to live together and love one another (5/7).

Health

Sickness brings pain and misery (9/5). Christians believe that Jesus healed many people (4/12, 4/15) and in this way showed that God loves people and wants them to be well and happy.

Justice

Christians believe that God is on the side of justice (1/17). Everyone is equally important (2/6) and to act greedily and unfairly is wrong (3/7). One day, Christians believe, God will put an end to all injustice for ever (5/19, 10/6, 10/20).

Love

Christians believe that God made the world and loves it (10/6). They believe that the good and right way to live is to respond to that love, by loving God and other people (1/19). They believe that Jesus shows God's love in action (volume 4) and is a model for how they should love one another (5/7, 5/10).

Money

A number of stories in the Bible show that as people grow rich they are easily tempted to use their money selfishly. They can be cruel to others in their greed to get even more money (3/1, 3/7). Jesus made it clear that people have to choose between putting God or money first in their lives (4/14). The first Christians were enthusiastic about sharing their wealth so that everyone's needs were met (5/2).

Peace

Peace happens when relationships are good. Christians believe that Jesus came to bring peace in all types of relationships: between people and God: between people and their fellow human beings; and between people and the world they live in. Volume 4 is all about Jesus: see especially 4/8, 4/9 and 4/10.

Poverty

The Bible shows how much God cares for people who are poor. One of the most important stories in the Old Testament is about God making it possible for the Israelites to escape from being poor slaves in Egypt. God helped them make their home in a new land, and gave them laws to remind them to treat everyone fairly (1/14–1/20: 2/1–2/6 and 9/5). Jesus said that God had a special concern for the poor. He also said that the poor were more likely to see their need of God than the rich, who were too comfortable to care about right and wrong (4/8).

Power

The Bible stories show that people who become greedy for power soon begin to treat others badly (3/1, 3/4, 3/7). This is not God's way. God rescued the Israelites when they were helpless slaves (1/17). Jesus became a friend of those who were poor and weak and powerless: it is people like these, who can recognize their need for God, who are on the right path (4/7, 4/13).

Violence

Some of the oldest stories in the Bible say that people are violent to one another and the world they live in because they have turned away from God (1/3, 1/4). Jesus let himself be arrested and put to death rather than fight back, and forgave those who had hurt him even as he hung dying on the cross (4/18). Christians believe that God is on the side of love and justice (10/6) and that anyone who asks for God's forgiveness and a new start will be helped to live in a peaceful, loving and right way (10/17).

Work

The Bible stories of the beginning say that God made one day in seven to be a day of rest (1/2) and commanded people to keep it (1/19). Forcing people to work too hard is cruel and wrong (1/14, 3/1), but having work to do and so being able to make a living is a good thing (2/6, 8/10). The first Christians included many who worked very hard spreading the news about Jesus (5/16).

SPECIAL ASSIGNMENT

SUPER SLEUTH

To look up any topic, brainstorm all the words that help describe it. For example, if you wanted to know more about weddings in Bible times you might think of wedding, husband, wife, and the names of Bible people who are described as getting married: Isaac, Rebekah, Jacob, Rachel. Then look up each of these words in the index. Some of the pages listed will in fact only say a little bit about the topic you are researching. Others will tell you a great deal.

Some will suggest to you new words that perhaps you didn't know before that you can add to your list of things to look up: in the case of a wedding, you might go on to look up more about a dowry or music.

If you are doing research for a big project (rather than just browsing for fun), make notes of all the pages that you find helpful so you can look them up again and note down the information you want from them.

Superquiz

Do you know which of the suggested answers is the right one in this superquiz? If not, you can sleuth the answer in Bible World.

Decide which of the words in the question are the important ones.

Look them up in the index, and then turn to the pages listed. On one of them you will eventually find the answer to the question.

1　In the story of Noah, the first bird let out of the ark was a

raven

dove

eagle

2　Jacob had a twin brother named

Abel

Esau

Benjamin

3　Who won a battle by blowing trumpets, smashing pots and waving torches?

Joshua

Gideon

Saul

4　David's clever trick to capture the city he renamed Jerusalem was to

kill the giant protecting it with a stone from a slingshot

send his men up the water tunnel into the city

play the harp every day for seven days so the walls fell down

5　Who asked God to set a water-drenched altar alight?

Abraham

Moses

Elijah

6　Which temple in Jerusalem stood the longest? The one built by

Solomon

Zerubbabel

Herod

7　Jesus once described the relationship between himself and his followers like this. 'I am the vine, you are the

leaves

grapes

branches

8　The stories of the last Passover Jesus ate with his disciples tells of them sharing

bread and wine

loaves and fishes

water that became wine

9　The first person to be put to death for being a Christian was

Judas Iscariot

Stephen

Paul

10　A lot of the letters in the New Testament were written by

Paul

Matthew

Luke

11　The first five books of the Hebrew Bible (the Christian Old Testament) are sometimes called

the books of Moses

the Septuagint

the books of wisdom

12　Three of the four Gospels are quite similar to each other. The odd one out is

Matthew

Mark

Luke

John

13　Which of the following Bible-times animals is now extinct in Israel?

wolf

leopard

lion

14　Jesus' home town of Nazareth is

in the hills of Galilee

on the shore of Lake Galilee

just outside Jerusalem

15　In the farming year of Bible times, one of the last crops to be harvested was

flax

grain

olives

16　In Bible times, arrangements for people to marry were usually made

when they were about 7 or 8

when they were about 12 or 13

when they were about 18 or 19

17 Synagogues became the places where people met to worship

when they settled the land of Canaan and no longer had a camp with a tabernacle at the centre

when Solomon built a temple and they could not all travel to Jerusalem

when Solomon's temple was destroyed and the people were taken to a foreign land to live

18 In the time of Jesus people had to pay taxes to

the Assyrians

the Babylonians

the Romans

19 The word angel means

messenger

shining one

young woman

20 The word Christ means

God with us

anointed one

Saviour

Answers

1   raven
2   Esau
3   Gideon
4   send his men up the water tunnel into the city
5   Elijah
6   Zerubbabel
7   branches
8   bread and wine
9   Stephen
10 Paul
11 the books of Moses
12 John
13 lion
14 in the hills of Galilee
15 olives
16 when they were about 12 or 13
17 when Solomon's temple was destroyed and the people were taken to a foreign land to live
18 the Romans
19 messenger
20 anointed one

 # True or False?

1   Moses was for several years a shepherd.

2   Mount Zion is another word for heaven.

3   There is a story about Daniel being thrown into a fiery furnace because he refused to worship the statue of a foreign god.

4   According to the Bible, when Jesus was born, Herod the Great was king in Jerusalem.

5   The apostle Paul was a Christian from the time he was a little boy.

6   The most recent Bible books were written nearly 2000 years ago.

7   The River Jordan links Lake Galilee and the Dead Sea.

8   Jesus probably never went to school.

9   The gate was the weakest point in the defences of the walled cities of Canaan.

10 In the Bible, angels are always described as shining brightly.

Answers

1 True.

2 False. It is the hill in Jerusalem where the temple stood.

3 False. The book of Daniel has a story of three young men being thrown into a furnace.

There is a different story about Daniel being thrown into a lion's den.

4 True. Matthew's story of the wise men coming to visit Jesus says they first went to visit King Herod, thinking he would know about a new king.

5 False. He was a young man well known for trying to get rid of Christians... but he was suddenly converted.

6 True.

7 True.

8 False. He probably went to the local synagogue school when he was a boy.

9 True.

10 False. Some seem to shine brightly: others look like ordinary people.

Index

A

Aaron 1/15, 1/16; 9/3
Abednego 3/14
Abel 1/1, 1/3, 1/4
Abraham 1/1, 1/7, 1/8, 1/9, 1/10, 1/11, 1/13, 1/15, 1/20; 3/12; 5/7; 6/1; 7/1, 7/13, 7/18; 8/2; 9/1, 9/7, 9/8, 9/19, 9/20; 10/20
Absalom 2/17
Acts, book of 5/1, 5/16; 6/13
Adam 1/1, 1/3, 1/6; 6/2; 7/2
Adriatic Sea 7/19
Aegean Sea 5/18; 7/19
Africa 6/15; 7/3
Africa, East 2/18
Ahab 3/2, 3/3, 3/4, 3/5, 3/6, 3/7; 6/6; 7/14; 9/8, 9/9
Ahaz 3/8, 3/9
Ahaziah 3/4
Aijalon 2/14
Akkad, Akkadian 3/11; 7/2
Alexander (Herod's son) 4/5
Alexander II of Russia 10/4
Alexander the Great 3/20; 4/1; 6/1, 6/10; 7/19; 9/8
Alexandria 6/10; 7/3
almond blossom 8/6
alphabet 2/3; 6/3
altar 2/19; 3/3, 3/10; 4/3; 6/11; 10/12, 10/16
Amalekites 2/2, 2/7
Amarna letters 2/1
Ammonites 2/2, 2/14
Amnon 7/17
Amon 3/10
Amos 3/7, 3/8; 6/6; 9/6, 9/10
amphitheatre 5/5, 5/9
Ananias 5/4
Anat 2/3
Andrew 4/7
Andronicus 5/16
angel 1/10; 2/8; 3/14, 3/16; 4/3, 4/4, 4/5, 4/19; 5/10, 5/14, 5/19; 10/1, 10/9, 10/12, 10/14
Angel of Death 8/8
animal, animals 5/5; 7/6, 7/10, 7/12, 7/14; 8/12, 8/13, 8/14, 8/16, 8/17
anointed, anointing 2/13, 2/16; 4/3
Antioch (in Pisidia) 5/6, 5/8
Antioch (in Syria) 5/1, 5/3, 5/6, 5/7, 5/8, 5/9; 7/18; 10/13
Antiochus IV 3/20; 4/1
Antipater 4/5
Antonia, Fort of 5/12; 7/15; 9/4
Apocrypha 6/11
apostle 5/16, 5/20; 6/1
Apsu 10/5
aqueduct 8/3
Aquila 5/9, 5/16
Arabah Valley 7/12
Arabs, Arabia 1/1, 1/8; 2/18; 5/2; 7/6, 7/17; 9/19

Aramaic 3/16; 4/6; 6/3, 6/9, 6/13, 6/16; 8/12; 9/11
Ararat 7/18
archaeology, archaeologist 1/7, 1/14; 2/5; 6/3; 8/13; 10/1, 10/2, 10/3, 10/4, 10/5
archbishop 6/18
Archelaus 4/6
archer 3/6, 3/16; 9/8, 9/9
Arimathea 4/18
Aristobulus 4/5
ark (Noah's) 1/4; 7/18
ark (synagogue) 6/4; 9/11
ark of the covenant see covenant box
Armenian 6/16
armour 4/2; 9/8
army 1/7, 1/17; 2/6, 2/7, 2/8, 2/13, 2/14, 2/18; 3/5, 3/6, 3/12, 3/16; 4/1, 4/2, 4/7, 4/13; 5/5; 6/11; 9/1, 9/7, 9/8, 9/9, 9/11, 9/12; 10/8
arrest 4/17, 4/18; 5/3, 5/4, 5/12, 5/13
arrow 8/13; 9/8
Artemis 5/9
Ashdod 2/9, 2/13, 2/14; 7/7
Asher 1/11; 2/6
Asherah 2/3
Ashkelon 2/9, 2/13, 2/14
Ashtoreth 2/9, 2/12
Ashurbanipal 3/6
Asia 5/2, 5/6, 5/8, 5/12, 5/13, 5/16; 6/14, 6/15
Asia Minor 2/1; 7/1, 7/18
ass 9/12

Assyria, Assyrian 2/1; 3/5, 3/6, 3/7, 3/8, 3/9, 3/10, 3/11, 3/16, 3/17, 3/19; 6/5, 6/6; 7/2, 7/8, 7/18; 9/3, 9/6, 9/7, 9/8, 9/9, 9/14; 10/3, 10/8, 10/12, 10/20
Astarte 2/3
astrologer 4/5
astronomy 3/11
Aswan 7/3
Athena 5/8
Athens 3/20; 4/1, 4/2; 5/1, 5/8; 7/19; 10/8
Atonement, Day of 1/20; 2/19; 4/3; 8/7; 9/2
Atrahasis 1/5
Attalia 5/6
Augustus Caesar 4/1, 4/4, 4/5; 5/15, see also Emperor, Roman
aunt 8/1
authority 6/19
autumn 7/5

B

Baal 2/3, 2/12; 3/2, 3/3, 3/4, 3/5; 10/8
Baalzebul 2/9
Babel, tower of 3/11; 7/2
baby 8/11
Babylon, Babylonia, Babylonian, Babylonians, Babylonian Empire 1/1, 1/4, 1/6, 1/7, 1/11; 2/2; 3/6, 3/10, 3/11, 3/12, 3/13, 3/14, 3/15, 3/16, 3/17; 6/3, 6/5, 6/6, 6/7, 6/9, 6/10, 6/19; 7/2, 7/15, 7/18; 9/2, 9/6, 9/8, 9/10, 9/11, 9/13; 10/1, 10/3, 10/5, 10/8, 10/12, 10/16, 10/20
baker 1/13
ball 8/13
bandit 9/12
Baniyas see Caesarea Philippi
Baptist, John the 4/3, 4/7, 4/13
baptize, baptism 4/7; 5/1, 5/5, 5/6, 5/18; 10/17
bar mitzvah 6/1
Barak 2/7
barley 8/6, 8/12, 8/15
Barnabas 5/6, 5/7, 5/8, 5/16; 6/12; 10/13
barter 9/15
Bashan 7/17
basket 1/15
bath 8/5, 8/19
Bathsheba 2/17
battering ram 9/9
battle 2/5, 2/7, 2/8, 2/13, 2/14, 2/15, 2/16; 3/4, 3/6; 8/13
bear 7/12
beard 8/19
bedroom 8/4, 8/5
Beersheba 7/8
belt 8/18
Benjamin 1/11, 1/13
Benjamin (tribe of) 2/6, 2/13; 7/14
Berea 5/8
Bes 1/12
Bethany 4/16; 7/16
Bethel 2/5; 3/2, 3/7; 10/8
Bethlehem 2/11; 4/3, 4/4, 4/5, 4/20; 5/1; 6/12; 7/14, 7/16; 8/16; 10/14
Bethsaida 4/8
Bilhah 1/11
bird, birds 5/5; 8/11, 8/13; 7/5; 10/7
birth 10/14
bishop 6/15
Bithynia 5/2
Black Sea 7/1
blessing 1/8, 1/9, 1/10; 8/11; 10/13, 10/18
blind 4/12, 4/13
blood 1/17
boar, wild 7/10, 7/12
boat 1/4; 3/11, 3/19; 9/13
Boaz (pillar of temple) 2/19
Boaz (relative of Ruth) 2/11
body 10/19

bone, bones 3/13; 8/19
Booths, festival of 8/7
bow 8/13; 9/8
boy 8/9, 8/12
bread 1/17; 4/7, 4/9, 4/11, 4/13, 4/17; 5/10;
  8/4, 8/8, 8/14, 8/15, 8/16; 10/16
breakfast 8/16
brick, bricks 1/6, 1/12, 1/14; 3/11, 3/16; 7/3;
  8/5
bride 8/9
bridegroom 8/9
bridesmaid 8/9
bronze 1/18; 9/1, 9/19
Bronze Age 7/18; 10/1, 10/2
brother 8/1, 8/19
builder 4/6; 10/15
Bulgaria 7/1
bull 3/2, 3/3, 3/6; 10/8
bush (burning) 1/16
business 9/14
butler 1/13
Byblos 9/13

C

Caananites 7/7
Caesarea (maritime) 4/2, 4/5, 4/18; 5/3, 5/5,
  5/8, 5/12, 5/13; 6/13; 7/7
Caesarea Philippi 4/8; 5/1; 7/8, 7/9
Caiaphas 4/18
Cain 1/1, 1/3, 1/4
Cairo 7/3
calendar 3/11; 8/6
calf 1/19
camel, camels 7/6; 9/12
campsite 8/2
Camyses 3/16
Cana 7/9
Canaan, Canaanite, Canaanites 1/1, 1/7, 1/8,
  1/9, 1/10, 1/11, 1/12, 1/13, 1/17, 1/19; 2/1,
  2/2, 2/3, 2/4, 2/6, 2/9, 2/11, 2/13, 2/14, 2/17;
  3/2, 3/3, 3/7, 3/9; 6/3; 7/1, 7/15, 7/17; 8/1,
  8/2, 8/3, 8/7; 9/1, 9/4, 9/8, 9/9, 9/18
canoe 9/13
Capernaum 4/8; 5/1; 7/9; 8/4; 9/11
caravan 9/12
Carmel, Mount 3/2, 3/3; 4/5; 7/7, 7/14
carpenter 9/17; 10/15 see also builder
carriage 9/12
cart 9/12
Carthage 6/15
carving 3/6
casemate wall 9/9
catacombs 7/20
catapult 4/2
cave 6/9; 10/4
cedar 2/18, 2/19; 9/17
cedar wood 7/7, 7/11
centurian 4/2
ceramic index 10/2
Chaldea 1/7
Champollion, Jean-François 10/3
chapel 1/7

chapter 6/18
chariot, chariots 1/13, 1/17; 2/6, 2/7, 2/18; 3/5,
  3/6; 4/2; 9/8, 9/12
charismatic gifts 5/10
cheese 8/15, 8/16
cherubim 2/19
child, children 2/12; 3/7; 4/13, 4/14, 4/15;
  5/10, 5/18, 5/20; 6/8, 6/17; 8/1, 8/2, 8/9, 8/10;
  10/6, 10/7, 10/9, 10/10, 10/13, 10/14, 10/15,
  10/17, 10/19
chi-rho 5/20
Christ 4/4; 6/12; 7/8; 10/11, 10/14, see also
  Jesus
Christianity 6/1, 6/11, 6/15, 6/16; 7/1, 7/19
Christians 1/19; 5/1, 5/2, 5/3, 5/4, 5/5, 5/6, 5/7,
  5/8, 5/9, 5/10, 5/11, 5/12, 5/13, 5/14, 5/15,
  5/16, 5/17, 5/18, 5/19, 5/20; 6/12, 6/13, 6/14,
  6/15, 6/16, 6/17, 6/18, 6/19, 6/20; 7/18, 7/19,
  7/20
Christmas 4/4
Chronicles, 1 and 2 6/5
church 5/1, 5/2, 5/3, 5/6, 5/7, 5/9, 5/10, 5/14,
  5/16, 5/17, 5/18;
  6/14, 6/15, 6/18, 6/20
Cilicia 2/18; 5/4, 5/13; 9/8
circumcision 8/11
circus 4/2
cistern 8/3, 8/4, 8/5; 9/4
citizen 5/4, 5/8
city 2/3, 2/5, 2/6, 2/9, 2/14, 2/17; 8/3; 9/9,
  9/12; 10/8, 10/20
clan 8/1
clay 9/16
clay tablet 6/3; 10/5
climate 7/5
cloak 8/11, 8/18
cloth 8/10
clothes 8/17
coastlands 7/7
coat 1/11
cock 4/20
codex 6/3; 10/4
coin 9/15
colony (Roman) 5/8
Colossae 5/8, 5/14; 6/14
Colosseum 7/20
Colossians 6/14
commandment: see law
Commandments, Ten 3/4; 6/4
Constantine 6/16
cooking 8/4, 8/15
copper 2/18; 9/19
Coptic 6/16
Corinth 5/8, 5/9, 5/11, 5/16, 5/18; 6/14; 7/19;
  10/19
Corinthians 6/14
Corinthians, letter to 5/11
corn 3/7
Cornelius 5/5
Council, Jewish 5/3, 5/13
court 3/6
courtyard 1/7; 8/4, 8/10, 8/15
cousin 8/1

covenant 1/20, see also 4/17; 10/16
covenant box 1/18, 1/20; 2/13, 2/17, 2/18; 3/1,
  3/2, 3/12; 9/2; 10/8
cradle 4/4; 8/11, 8/16
craft workers 2/3, 2/17, 2/18, 2/19
creation 10/17, 10/18
creation story 1/2, 1/6
Crete 5/2, 5/13
crops 10/8, 10/16
cross 4/18; 10/13
crown 10/15
crown of thorns 4/18
crucifixion 4/18; 5/2, 5/4, 5/10, 5/11, 5/16,
  5/18; 9/4; 10/13, 10/19
cuneiform 6/3; 10/3, 10/5
cymbals 9/3
Cyprus 5/6, 5/8, 5/13
Cyrene 5/2
Cyrus 3/16, 3/17; 7/2

D

Dagon 2/9, 2/10
Damasus 6/16
Damascus 2/18; 3/6, 3/8, 3/11, 3/16; 5/4, 5/13;
  7/2, 7/9
Dan 1/11; 2/6; 3/2; 7/8; 10/8
dance 2/20; 9/3
dancing 8/8, 8/9
Daniel 3/14, 3/16, 3/20; 6/1, 6/6; 10/12, 10/19
Darius I 3/16; 10/3
date 8/6, 8/16
David 2/1, 2/4, 2/15, 2/16, 2/17, 2/18, 2/19; 3/1; 4/4;
  6/1, 6/5, 6/6; 7/6, 7/19; 8/13; 9/3, 9/6, 9/7, 9/8
deacon 5/3, 5/5
Dead Sea 1/10, 1/17; 6/9; 7/4, 7/12, 7/13; 10/4
deaf 4/12
death 1/16, 1/17, 1/18; 4/12, 4/13, 4/18, 4/19;
  5/2, 5/3, 5/4, 5/14, 5/16, 5/19, 5/20; 6/12;
  8/20; 10/9, 10/11, 10/15, 10/19
death penalty 9/4
Deborah 2/7
Decapolis 4/8; 5/1; 7/17
dedication 6/11
Dedication, festival of 8/7
Delilah 2/10
Demetrius 5/9
demon 10/1, 10/10, 10/11
Derbe 5/6, 5/8
desert 1/7, 1/16, 1/17; 2/16; 3/3, 3/15; 7/3, 7/6,
  7/13, 7/14, 7/15, 7/17, 7/18
Deuterocanonical books 6/11
Deuteronomy 1/20; 6/4
devil 4/9; 10/1, 10/10
Diana 5/9
dice 8/13
Dinah 1/11
disabled people 10/7
disciple, disciples 4/7, 4/11, 4/10; 5/1, 5/2,
  5/5, 5/16, 5/19; 6/9, 6/12; 8/8
disease 3/5
disobedience 1/3, 1/5, 1/6
divorce 8/10

14

doctor 5/16; 6/13; 9/5
Domitian 5/15, 5/19
donkey 9/12
dove 1/4; 10/17
dowry 8/9
drama 2/20; 6/17
dream 1/11, 1/13; 3/2; 5/5, 5/8; 10/12,
  see also vision
dress 8/9
drought 3/2, 3/3
drum 9/3
dyeing 8/17
dynasty 1/12

E

earthquake 5/8
Ecclesiastes 2/20; 6/8; 10/20
Eden, garden of 1/3; 6/2
Edom 7/17
Egypt, Egyptian, Egyptians 1/1, 1/7, 1/8, 1/11,
  1/12, 1/13, 1/14, 1/15, 1/16, 1/17, 1/18, 1/19,
  1/20; 2/1, 2/4, 2/6, 2/7, 2/9, 2/11, 2/13, 2/18, 2/19;
  3/1, 3/2, 3/3, 3/6, 3/9, 3/10, 3/11, 3/12, 3/16; 4/1,
  4/5; 5/2; 6/3, 6/4, 6/5, 6/8, 6/10, 6/16; 7/1, 7/2, 7/3,
  7/7, 7/9, 7/18; 8/1, 8/2, 8/3, 8/7, 8/8, 8/11, 8/13
  8/18; 9/1, 9/2, 9/7 9/12, 9/13, 9/19; 10/1, 10/3,
  10/6, 10/8, 10/11, 10/12, 10/19
Ekron 2/9, 2/13, 2/14
El 2/3
Elah, Valley of 2/15
Elam 5/2
Elath 7/12
Eli 2/10
Elijah 3/2, 3/3, 3/4; 6/6; 7/7; 9/10
Elimelech 2/11
Elisha 3/5; 7/17; 8/5; 9/10
Elizabeth 4/3; 10/9
embroidery 2/19; 8/17
Emmaus 4/19
Emperor, Roman 3/6, 3/8, 3/11, 3/12, 3/16;
  4/1, 4/2, 4/4, 4/5; 5/13, 5/14, 5/15, 5/16, 5/19;
  7/8, *see also* Augustus Caesar, Hadrian,
  Titus, Nero, Domitian
empire 1/1, 1/12; 2/18; 3/6, 3/9, 3/11, 3/16,
  3/19, 3/20; 4/1, 4/2, 4/7; 9/1; 10/1, 10/3,
  10/16, *see also* Roman, Assyrian,
  Babylonian, Persian, Greek
En Gedi 2/16
Enuma Elish 10/5
environment 1/2, 1/3; 2/20; 4/9; 10/6, 10/10
Epaphras 5/14
Ephesians, letter to 5/14; 6/14
Ephesus 5/8, 5/9, 5/12, 5/14, 5/18; 6/13, 6/14,
  6/15; 7/18
Ephraim 2/6; 7/14
Epic of Gilgamesh 1/5
Erasmus 6/18
Esau 1/9, 1/10; 7/17
Esdradon, Vale of 7/7
Esther 3/16; 6/5; 8/7
Ethiopia, Ethiopian 5/1, 5/3
eucharist 4/17

Eunice 6/1
Euphrates, River 3/9, 3/11; 6/3; 7/1, 7/2
Eve 1/1, 1/3, 1/6; 6/2; 7/2
evil 1/6, 1/18; 6/14; 10/10
exile 3/6, 3/8, 3/12, 3/13, 3/14, 3/15; 6/5, 6/9;
  8/7; 9/11
exodus 1/17; 2/1
Exodus, book of 1/20; 6/4
Ezekiel 3/13, 3/15, 3/20; 6/6; 9/10; 10/12
Ezion-geber 2/18
Ezra 3/19; 6/5, 6/9

F

faith 5/6, 5/7, 5/9, 5/11, 5/12, 5/13, 5/17, 5/20;
  6/1, 6/2, 6/14, 6/20; 10/9, 10/16, 10/20
Faiyum 1/12
fallen (Fall) 10/10, 10/11
fallow year 8/6
family 8/1, 8/4, 8/5, 8/6, 8/9, 8/10, 8/11; 9/1
famine 1/7, 1/8, 1/13; 5/7
farm, farmer, farming 1/3; 6/6; 6/4; 7/9, 7/10,
  7/12, 7/14, 7/17, 7/18, 7/19, 7/20; 8/6, 8/10,
  8/14; 10/8
father 8/1, 8/2, 8/9, 8/12
Felix 5/13
fertile crescent 1/7, 1/12; 2/2; 7/1, 7/2, 7/3, 7/18
festival 1/20; 2/12, 2/19; 3/9, 3/10, 3/11, 3/16;
  4/3; 6/5, 6/9, 6/11; 8/7, 8/8; 10/5
figs 7/5; 8/4, 8/6, 8/16
fire 3/3; 5/2, 5/17
First fruits, festival of 8/7
firstborn 8/11
fish 8/14
fish symbol 7/20
fishermen, fishing 4/6, 4/7, 4/9, 4/10; 7/9, 7/11
flax 1/12; 8/4, 8/6, 8/10, 8/17, 8/18
fleece 2/8; 8/17, 8/18
flocks 8/2
flood 1/4, 1/5, 1/6; 7/2, 7/3, 7/5
flood stories 1/5
flour 8/14, 8/15, 8/16
flowers 7/5, 7/6, 7/10, 7/14
flute 8/20; 9/3
food 3/14; 5/7; 8/4, 8/14
foreigner, foreigners 2/11; 9/5; 10/6
forests 7/7, 7/12, 7/14, 7/19, 7/20
forgiveness 4/11, 4/17, 4/18, 4/20; 5/20; 6/6;
  10/13, 10/15
fort 4/5
fortifications 3/9; 8/3
fortress 9/9; 10/7
Francis of Assisi 6/19
frankincense 4/5
freedom 2/1, 2/2
freedom fighter 4/1, *see also* Zealots
frogs 1/16
fruit 7/5, 7/9; 8/6
fruit, forbidden 1/3
fuller 8/17
funeral 8/13, 8/20; 10/20
furnace 3/14; 9/19
furniture 2/3; 8/4, 8/5

G

Gabriel 4/3
Gad 1/11; 2/6; 7/17
Galatia 5/6, 5/8, 5/13; 6/14
Galatians, letter to 5/6, 5/12; 6/14
Galilee, area 3/2; 4/6, 4/16; 5/1; 7/9, 7/10; 10/2
Galilee, Lake 4/6, 4/7, 4/8, 4/9, 4/11, 4/12; 7/4,
  7/8, 7/9, 7/11, 7/12, 7/13
Gamaliel 5/3
game board 3/11
games 8/13
Gamla 4/2; 10/2
garden 3/4, 3/6, 3/11, 3/15
garden of Eden 1/3
Garstang, John 10/1
gate 4/13; 9/9
Gath 2/9, 2/13, 2/14
Gaza 2/9, 2/13, 2/14; 7/7
gazelle 7/6, 7/12
Geb 1/12
Gehenna 10/20
Genesis 1/2; 6/4; 10/17
Gentile, Gentiles 5/2, 5/5, 5/6, 5/7, 5/8, 5/12,
  5/20; 6/10, 6/13; 8/15
Georgian 6/16
Gerasa 7/17
Gethsemane, Garden of 4/17; 7/16; 10/9
Gezer 2/14; 7/8; 9/9
Gibeah 2/14
Gideon 2/8, 2/10; 9/6; 10/9
gifts, spiritual 5/10
Gilboa, Mount 2/14, 2/16
Gilead 7/17
Gilgal 2/14; 3/7
Gilgamesh, Epic of 1/5
girl 8/9, 8/12
glass 8/5
Gnostics 6/15
goat, goats 7/6, 7/14; 8/2, 8/7, 8/12
god, gods, goddess, goddesses 1/11, 1/12,
  1/18; 2/3, 2/9, 2/10, 2/18; 3/2, 3/3, 3/7, 3/9,
  3/10, 3/11, 3/14, 3/19, 3/20; 4/2; 5/1, 5/8, 5/9,
  5/11, 5/14; 10/5, 10/8
God-fearers 5/5
Golan Heights *see* Bashar
gold 1/9, 1/17, 1/18, 1/19; 2/18, 2/19; 3/1, 3/2,
  3/5, 3/12; 4/3, 4/5; 6/8; 9/19; 10/8, 10/20
Golgotha 4/18
Goliath 2/15
Gomer 3/7
Gomorrah 7/13
Goshen 1/17
gospel 4/5; 5/16, 5/18, 5/20; 6/1, 6/12, 6/13,
  6/14, 6/15; 10/14
Gothic 6/16
government 9/1, 9/7
governor 3/17, 3/18; 5/6, 5/13; 8/3
grain 8/3, 8/4, 8/5, 8/6, 8/14
grandparent 8/1
grapes 8/6, 8/14, 8/16
grapevines 7/5, 7/14, 7/17
grave 4/19; 8/19

Greek, Greeks, Greece 2/1, 2/9; 3/16, 3/20; 4/1, 4/6; 5/1, 5/5, 5/8, 5/9, 5/11, 5/12; 6/3, 6/10, 6/11, 6/13, 6/15, 6/16, 6/18; 7/1, 7/2, 7/17, 7/18, 7/19; 8/3, 8/12, 8/13, 8/18; 9/6, 9/8; 10/3, 10/8, 10/9, 10/17
Greek Empire 4/1; 6/1, 6/10, 6/18
guardian angel 10/9
guest 8/2, 8/16
Gutenberg 6/18

H

Habakkuk 6/6
Hadad 2/3
Hadrian 7/18
Hagar 1/8
Haggai 3/17; 6/6
hail 1/16
hairstyles 8/19
Huleh, Valley 7/8
Haman 3/16
Hammurabi, Hammurapi 3/11; 7/2
Hannah 2/12; 10/13
Hannukah, festival of 6/11; 8/7
Haran 1/7
harbours 7/11

harp 2/15, 2/16; 3/15; 8/13; 9/3
harvest 1/3, 1/13; 2/2, 2/11, 2/12; 5/2; 7/3, 7/5; 8/6, 8/12
Hazor 2/5, 2/7; 7/8; 9/9; 10/1
head-dress 8/9
healing 4/12; 5/3, 5/8, 5/10, 5/20; 10/2, 10/11, 10/15, 10/17
health 9/5
hearth 8/4, 8/15
heaven 1/6; 2/19; 4/8; 5/3, 5/19, 5/20; 10/8, 10/13, 10/14, 10/20
Hebrew 2/1, 2/7; 3/14, 3/16; 4/3, 4/6; 6/1, 6/3, 6/4, 6/9, 6/10, 6/13, 6/15; 8/12; 9/11; 10/4, 10/5
Hebrews, 'letter' to 5/17; 6/14
Hebron 1/10; 7/14, 7/15
hell 10/20
helmet 2/9; 4/2; 9/8
Hera 3/20
herb 8/8, 8/15, 8/16
Hermon, Mount 7/8, 7/13
Herod Agrippa 5/13
Herod Antipas 4/6, 4/13; 7/9, 9/10
Herod the Great 3/17; 4/1, 4/2, 4/5, 4/6, 4/19; 5/5, 5/12; 7/1, 7/7, 7/13, 7/15; 8/5, 8/8, 8/19; 9/2, 9/6, 9/9, 9/18; 10/16
Hezekiah 3/8, 3/9, 3/10; 10/3
hieroglyph, hieroglyphics 1/12; 2/3; 6/3, 6/16

high places 2/3
High Priest 2/19; 4/3, 4/20; 9/2, 9/3, 9/4
hills 7/4
hippopotamus 7/12
Hiram, King 2/18, 2/19
history 6/1, 6/2, 6/5, 6/19
Hittite, Hittites 1/1, 1/20; 2/1; 3/11; 7/18
Holocaust 10/10
Holy City 7/1
Holy Communion 4/17
Holy Land 7/1
Holy of holies 2/19; 4/3; 8/7
Holy Place 5/16
Holy Spirit 3/17; 4/7, 4/20; 5/2, 5/10, 5/20; 8/7
home, homes 2/3, 2/9; 8/3, 8/4, 8/5
honey 8/14, 8/15
hope 10/20
Horeb, Mount 1/19
horse, horses 2/18; 9/8, 9/12
horsemen 10/12
Hosea 3/5, 3/7; 6/5; 9/10; 10/20
Hoshea 3/8
hospitality 8/2
house 8/3, 8/4, 8/13
household 8/1
Huldah 3/10
Huleh, Lake 7/4, 7/13
hungry 4/8, 4/9, 4/11
husband 3/7, 3/8, 3/19; 8/1, 8/9
Hyksos 1/14
hymn 5/8; 6/7

I

Iconium 5/6, 5/8
idol 1/18, 1/19; 10/8
illness 7/9; 9/5
Immanuel 10/14
incarnation 10/14
incense 4/3
India 3/16; 4/1; 6/16
industry 2/18
Ingathering, festival of 8/7
injustice 10/5, 10/6, 10/10
ink 5/11; 9/7
inn 8/16
inscription 10/3
insects 1/16
inspired, inspiration 6/1, 6/19
Iran 6/16; 7/1
Iraq 7/1, 7/2; 10/1
Iris 3/20
iron 2/9; 7/18; 9/1, 9/19
Iron Age 9/19; 10/2
Isaac 1/1, 1/8, 1/9, 1/11, 1/20
Isaiah 3/8, 3/9, 3/15, 3/20; 6/6; 9/10; 10/12
Ishmael 1/8
Ishtar 3/11
Islam 6/1; 7/1
Israel 1/10, 1/11; 6/5
Israel (northern kingdom of) 3/1, 3/2, 3/3, 3/4, 3/5, 3/6, 3/7, 3/8, 3/19
Israelites 1/4-3/14; 6/1, 6/3; 7/1

Issachar 1/11; 2/6
Italy 5/1, 5/12, 5/13; 7/1, 7/20
ivory 8/5, 8/13

J

Jabbok, River 1/10; 7/4, 7/17
Jabesh-gilead 2/14
Jabin 2/2, 2/7; 7/8
Jachin 2/19
jackals 7/12
Jacob 1/1, 1/9, 1/10, 1/11, 1/13, 1/14, 1/15, 1/20; 7/17; 9/1; 10/12-
Jaffa 7/7
jail see prison
Jairus 4/12
James 6/12
James (brother of Jesus) 4/11
James (brother of John) 5/16
James (disciple) 4/7, 4/13
James (leader of the church in Jerusalem) 5/7, 5/16, 5/17
James, letter of 6/14
javelin 3/6
Jebel Musa 1/19
Jebus 2/17, see also Jerusalem
Jehoahaz 3/10
Jehoiachin 3/12, 3/14, 3/17
Jehoiakim 3/10, 3/12; 9/10
Jehu 3/5, 3/6, 3/7; 7/17
Jeremiah 3/12; 6/6; 9/4, 9/10; 10/12
Jericho 2/3, 2/4, 2/5; 4/8, 4/10; 5/1; 7/12, 7/17; 10/11
Jeroboam 3/1, 3/2, 9/7
Jeroboam II 3/7, 3/8
Jerome 6/16
Jerusalem 2/14, 2/17, 2/18, 2/19, 2/20; 3/1, 3/2, 3/6, 3/9, 3/10, 3/11, 3/12, 3/14, 3/15, 3/16, 3/17, 3/18, 3/19; 4/1, 4/2, 4/5, 4/6, 4/7, 4/8, 4/10, 4/15, 4/16; 5/1, 5/2, 5/3, 5/4, 5/5, 5/7, 5/8, 5/9, 5/12, 5/13, 5/16, 5/18, 5/20; 6/4, 6/6, 6/7, 6/9, 6/13, 6/19; 7/1, 7/2, 7/4, 7/5, 7/7, 7/14, 7/15, 7/16, 7/19, 7/20; 8/5, 8/8, 8/17; 9/9; 10/1, 10/3, 10/4, 10/12, 10/16
Jesus 2/4, 2/12, 2/17; 4/1-4/20; 5/1, 5/2, 5/3, 5/4, 5/5, 5/6, 5/7, 5/8, 5/9, 5/10, 5/11, 5/13; 6/1, 6/2, 6/12, 6/13, 6/14, 6/15, 6/17, 6/20; 7/1, 7/8, 7/9, 7/15, 7/16, 7/18, 7/19; 9/2, 9/7, 9/11, 9/20; 10/6, 10/7, 10/9, 10/11, 10/13, 10/14, 10/15, 10/16, 10/17, 10/18, 10/19, 10/20
jewellery 1/9, 1/17, 1/18; 2/3; 8/9, 8/18; 9/19
jewels 10/20
Jews, Jewish people (especially) 1/8, 1/16, 1/17, 1/19; 3/14, 3/15, 3/16, 3/17, 3/19, 3/20; 5/1, 5/2, 5/3, 5/4, 5/5, 5/6, 5/7, 5/9, 5/10, 5/12, 5/16, 5/20; 6/1, 6/4, 6/9, 6/10, 6/12, 6/13, 6/17; 8/5, 8/12, 8/15; 10/5, 10/10, 10/16
Jezebel 3/2, 3/4, 3/5
Jezreel 3/4; 7/14
Job 6/8; 10/20
Jochebed 1/5
Joel 5/2; 6/6

16

John (disciple) 4/7, 4/13, 4/20; 5/3, 5/16; 6/12

John, Gospel of 5/18, 5/20; 6/12, 6/13, 6/15; 10/14

John, letters of 5/18; 6/14; 10/6

John the Baptist 2/10; 4/3, 4/7, 4/13; 10/2, 10/9, 10/16

Jonah 3/19; 6/6

Jonathan 2/16

Jones, Mary 6/19

Joppa 2/18; 3/19; 5/5; 7/7

Joram 3/4, 3/5

Jordan, River 1/10, 1/17; 2/1, 2/4, 2/6, 2/14; 3/2, 3/5; 4/7; 5/4, 5/5; 7/1, 7/4, 7/6, 7/8, 7/9, 7/12, 7/13, 7/17; 10/11

Jordan Valley 7/12

Joseph 1/11, 1/13, 1/14; 6/1; 7/3, 7/9; 8/2, 8/18; 9/7; 10/12, 10/14

Joseph (husband of Mary) 4/4, 4/6; 8/16

Joseph of Arimathea 4/18, 4/19

Joshua (Moses' successor) 2/2, 2/3, 2/4, 2/5, 2/6, 2/7, 2/20; 7/8, 7/19; 9/8; 10/11, 10/14

Joshua, book of 6/5

Joshua (priest) 3/17, 3/20

Josiah 3/10, 3/12; 6/5, 6/9

Jotham 3/8

Judah 1/11, 1/13; 2/6; 3/1, 3/2, 3/6, 3/8, 3/9, 3/10, 3/11, 3/12, 3/13, 3/14, 3/15, 3/16, 3/17; 4/3; 6/5, 6/6, 6/9; 7/2, 7/14; 9/6, 9/10, 9/11, 9/12; 10/3, 10/8

Judaism 6/1; 7/1

Judas (Iscariot) 4/17; 5/2, 5/16

Judas Maccabeus 4/1; 6/1, 6/11; 9/6, 9/8

Jude, letter of 5/18, 6/14

Judea 4/1, 4/2, 4/5, 4/7, 4/8; 5/1, 5/2, 5/4; 7/1, 7/6, 7/14

judge 1/6; 2/7, 2/8, 2/9, 2/10, 2/12, 2/13; 5/20; 8/3; 9/4, 9/6, 9/8

Judges, book of 6/5

Jum'a Muhammed 10/4

Junia 5/16

Jupiter 4/2

justice 1/4, 1/12; 2/6, 2/7, 2/9; 3/1, 3/2, 3/5, 3/7, 3/8, 3/9; 5/19, 5/20; 6/4, 6/6, 6/8; 9/2, 9/4, 9/14; 10/5, 10/6, 10/19

K

Kadesh-barnea 1/17

Kana see Cana

Khnum 1/12

kid (goat) 8/8

Kidron (brook) 7/16

kiln 9/15, 9/18

kilt 2/9; 8/18

Kineret, Lake see Galilee, Lake

king, kingdom 1/8, 1/11, 1/12, 1/16; 2/1, 2/3, 2/4, 2/6, 2/7, 2/13, 2/14, 2/15, 2/16, 2/17, 2/18; 3/1, 3/2, 3/3, 3/4, 3/6, 3/7, 3/8, 3/9, 3/10, 3/12, 3/13, 3/14, 3/16, 3/17, 3/18, 3/20; 4/1, 4/3, 4/4, 4/5, 4/16, 4/18, 4/19; 6/4, 6/5, 6/6, 6/9, 6/12; 8/3; 9/1, 9/6, 9/7, 9/8, 9/10, 9/15; 10/3, 10/6, 10/7, 10/8, 10/14

kingdom of God 2/12, 2/17; 4/3, 4/8, 4/10, 4/11, 4/14, 4/15, 4/16, 4/18; 10/14

Kings, books of (1 and 2) 6/5

Kingu 10/5

kinnor 2/16; 9/3

Kiriath Jearim 2/13

Kishon, River 2/7; 7/4

kitchen 8/4, 8/5

kohl 8/19

L

Laban 1/10

Lachish 2/5; 3/9; 6/3; 10/3

lamb 1/3, 1/17; 8/8; 10/16

lame 4/13

Lamech 1/4

lamp 5/20; 6/4; 8/4, 8/16; 9/16; 10/2

lampstand 4/3; 5/16; 9/2, 9/11

Langton, Stephen 6/18

language, languages 1/6; 5/2; 6/1

Laodicea 6/14, 6/15

Last Supper 4/17

Latin 4/6; 6/10, 6/12, 6/16, 6/18

law, laws 1/19, 1/20; 2/6, 2/11, 2/12, 2/13, 2/16, 2/19; 3/1, 3/2, 3/3, 3/4, 3/5, 3/7, 3/8, 3/10, 3/11, 3/12, 3/19, 3/20; 4/1, 4/5, 4/6, 4/10, 4/15; 5/3, 5/5, 5/7, 5/16; 6/1, 6/3, 6/4, 6/5, 6/6, 6/9, 6/10; 8/7, 8/8, 8/11, 8/15; 9/1, 9/2, 9/4, 9/5, 9/7, 9/10, 9/11, 9/15, 9/20; 10/6, 10/10, 10/15

Lazarus 4/12; 7/16

leader 2/1, 2/2, 2/6, 2/14

leaders (church) 5/6, 5/11, 5/12, 5/17, 5/18

Leah 1/10, 1/11

leather 8/2; 9/8, 9/20; 10/4

leatherworker 5/5, 5/6; 9/20

Lebanon 7/1

legionary 4/2

lentil 8/15

leopard 7/12

leprosy 4/11, 4/13

letter 3/16; 5/6, 5/11, 5/12, 5/14, 5/17; 6/1, 6/13, 6/14, 6/15; 10/6

Levi 1/11

Levite 9/3

Leviticus 1/20; 6/4

library 3/6; 10/4

Libya 5/2

life 4/12, 4/13, 4/14, 4/19

light 4/13; 6/19; 10/2

lightning 3/10

Lights, festival of 8/7

linen 1/12, 1/18; 8/17

lion 3/13, 3/16, 3/20; 5/15; 7/12, 7/20

locust 1/16

Lois 6/1

loom 2/10; 8/17, 8/18

Lord 10/14

'Lord', the 3/3, 3/13, 3/15, 3/20

Lord's prayer 4/11; 6/7; 10/13

Lot 1/7; 7/13; 10/9

love 6/4, 6/6, 6/7, 6/8, 6/12, 6/19, 6/20; 9/2; 10/5, 10/6, 10/17

Luke, Gospel of 4/3; 5/8, 5/16; 6/13, 6/15; 9/5; 5/16, 5/20; 10/14

Luther, Martin 6/18

Lydia 5/8; 6/13

lyre 9/3

Lystra 5/6, 5/8

M

Ma'at 1/12

Maccabees 4/1; 6/11

Maccabeus, Judas 4/1

Macedonia 3/16; 5/8, 5/13; 7/2, 7/19

Machaerus 4/5

Magdala 7/9, 7/11

magic 1/18; 10/5, 10/11

make-up 8/19

Malachi 3/18; 6/6

Malta 5/13

man 8/1, 8/10

Manasseh 2/6; 3/10; 7/14

manger 4/4

manuscript 6/9, 6/13, 6/19; 10/4, 10/5

Marduk 3/11; 10/5

Mariamne 4/5

Mark 4/6, 4/12; 5/8; 6/12, 6/13, 6/15; 10/14

Mark, Gospel of 5/20

market 5/6; 9/14

marriage 1/9; 3/7; 5/11, 5/16; 6/8; 8/9; 9/7

marshes 7/2, 7/7, 7/8

Martha 4/16; 7/16

martyr 5/3

Mary (mother of Jesus) 4/4, 4/5, 4/6; 7/16; 8/11, 8/16; 10/12, 10/13, 10/14

Mary (Magdalene) 4/18, 4/19; 7/9

Mary (sister of Martha) 4/16

Masada 7/13; 10/2

Mass 4/17
Matthew 4/4, 4/5; 6/13, 6/15; 10/14
Matthew, Gospel of 5/20
meal 8/16
meat 8/15, 8/16
Media 3/16; 5/2; 7/2
Mediterranean Sea 1/7, 1/17; 4/1, 4/2, 4/5; 5/1,
    5/2, 5/4, 5/6, 5/8, 5/13, 5/20; 6/12, 6/13, 6/14,
    6/15; 7/1, 7/2, 7/7, 7/8, 7/9, 7/12, 7/13, 7/18,
    7/19, 7/20; 9/12, 9/13
Megiddo 2/3; 7/7, 7/8; 8/3; 9/9
Memphis 1/12
men 8/1, 8/10
menorah 3/14
merchant 1/11
Merenptah 2/1
Meshach 3/14
Mesopotamia, Mesopotamian,
    Mesopotamians 2/1, 2/2, 2/18; 8/3; 10/1,
    10/3, 10/5
messenger 6/14
Messiah 3/20; 4/1, 4/3, 4/7, 4/9, 4/13, 4/16,
    4/18, 4/19; 5/2, 5/3, 5/4, 5/6, 5/7, 5/12, 5/13,
    5/20; 6/6, 6/12, 6/15, 6/20; 10/11,
    10/14
metals 7/18, 7/19
metalworker 9/19
Micah 3/8; 6/6
Middle Ages 6/17; 7/1, 7/2, 7/3, 7/18
Midianites 2/2, 2/7, 2/8
midwife 1/15
migration 7/5
military service 9/8
milk 8/2, 8/15
mill 8/4
miracle 4/7, 4/9, 4/12; 10/11
Miriam 1/15; 10/13
missionary 5/16
Moab, Moabites 2/2, 2/11
monastery 6/3, 6/16
money 9/15
monk 6/16, 6/18
monument 10/3
Mordecai 3/16
Moses 1/1, 1/15, 1/16, 1/17, 1/18, 1/19, 1/20;
    2/1, 2/2, 2/20; 3/1, 3/3, 3/4, 3/10; 6/1, 6/4,
    6/5; 7/17, 7/18; 9/3, 9/4; 10/6, 10/11, 10/13
mother 8/1, 8/2, 8/12
Mount Ararat 1/5
Mount of Olives 4/16
mourning 8/20
murder 1/3
music 2/16, 2/20; 3/14, 3/15; 8/9, 8/13; 9/3
musician 6/7
Myra 5/13
myrrh 4/5
mystery play 6/17

N

Nabateans 7/17
Nabopolassar 3/11
Naboth 3/4

Nahum 6/6
Namaan 3/5; 10/11
name 8/11
Naomi 2/11
Naphtali 1/11; 2/6
Napoleon 10/3
Nathan 2/17; 6/6
Nazareth 4/4, 4/6, 4/8; 5/1; 7/9; 10/15
Nazirite 2/10, 2/12
Nebo, Mount 7/17
Nebuchadnezzar, King 3/11, 3/12, 3/14, 3/17;
    6/9; 10/16
Negev 7/6, 7/14
Nehemiah 3/18; 6/5; 9/9; 10/13
Nero 5/13, 5/14, 5/15, 5/16, 5/17; 6/12
New Testament 1/20; 2/4; 4/6; 6/1, 6/3, 6/7,
    6/12, 6/13, 6/14, 6/15, 6/16, 6/18; 7/1
Nicanor 5/3
Nicodemus 4/14
Nicolaus 5/3
Nile, River 1/12, 1/15, 1/16, 1/17; 6/3; 7/1, 7/3
Nineveh 3/6, 3/9, 3/11, 3/19; 6/6; 7/2
Noah 1/1, 1/5, 1/6, 1/20; 6/17; 7/18

nomad, nomads 1/1, 1/7, 1/8; 7/6; 8/2, 8/7,
    8/16; 9/1, 9/7, 9/8
Numbers, book of 1/20; 6/4
Nut 1/12

O

oaks 7/7, 7/11, 7/14
Obadiah 6/6
oil 9/7
Old Testament 1/20; 2/16; 4/3, 4/6, 4/9; 6/1,
    6/2, 6/4, 6/5, 6/6, 6/7, 6/8, 6/9, 6/10, 6/11,
    6/15, 6/16; 7/1
olive oil 8/11, 8/14, 8/15, 8/19
olive trees 7/14, 7/16, 7/17
olive wood 2/19
olives 1/4; 8/6, 8/14, 8/16
Olives, Mount of 7/16
Omri 3/2, 3/4; 7/14
Onager 7/6
Onesimus 5/14; 6/15; 10/7
ore 9/19
oryx 7/6
ossuary 4/19; 8/19
outcasts 6/13
oven 8/4, 8/15
ox 9/12

P

Paddan-aram 1/7
painting 3/6; 6/17
palace 3/3, 3/4, 3/5, 3/6, 3/12; 8/3, 8/5; 10/3, 10/8

Palestine 3/20; 4/1, 4/2; 5/1, 5/4, 5/5, 5/12;
    6/13; 7/1, 7/19; 8/5, 8/10; 10/1, 10/14, 10/15
palm 4/16
Pamphylia 5/6
Pan 7/8
pan-pipes 8/19
Paphos 5/6
Papius 6/13
papyrus 1/15; 5/11; 6/3, 6/13; 7/3, 7/8
parable 4/10; 6/2, 6/12 see also story
parallelism 6/7
parent, parents 6/8; 8/11
park 8/15
Parmenas 5/3
Parthia 3/16; 5/2; 7/2
party 5/7, 5/10; 8/5, 8/9, 8/13; 10/7
Passover 1/17, 1/20
Passover, festival of 3/10; 4/16, 4/17; 5/2; 6/5;
    8/7, 8/8, 8/12
path 4/13
Patmos 5/19
Paul 5/4, 5/6, 5/7, 5/8, 5/11, 5/12, 5/13, 5/17,
    5/19; 6/1, 6/12, 6/13, 6/14, 6/15, 6/20; 7/18,
    7/19; 9/4; 10/8, 10/12, 10/13
peace 1/4; 2/6, 2/8, 2/20; 3/1, 3/9, 3/20; 6/5,
    6/6
pearly gates 10/20
Pekah 3/8
pen 5/11; 9/7
pencil case 5/11
Pentecost, festival of 1/20; 5/2, 5/5, 5/15, 5/20;
    8/7; 10/16
perfume 8/19
Perga 5/6
Pergamum 6/14
persecution 5/15, 5/16, 5/17; 6/12
Persepolis 3/16, 3/18; 7/2
Persia, Persian, Persians, Persian Empire 3/11,
    3/16, 3/17, 3/18; 6/5, 6/9, 6/10; 7/2, 7/18; 9/6,
    9/11; 10/3
Persian Gulf 7/1
Peshitta 6/16
pet 8/13
Peter 4/7, 4/8, 4/13, 4/14, 4/19, 4/20; 5/2, 5/3,
    5/5, 5/7, 5/15, 5/16; 6/12, 6/16, 6/20; 7/9; 8/4;
    10/12
Peter, letters of 5/17; 6/14
Petra 7/17
Petrie, William Flinders 10/2
pharaoh 1/12, 1/13, 1/14, 1/15, 1/16, 1/17,
    1/18; 6/10
Pharisee, Pharisees 4/1, 4/14; 10/19
Philadelphia 6/14; 7/17

Philemon, letter to 5/14; 6/14; 10/17
Philip 4/6; 5/1, 5/3, 5/5, 5/12
Philippi 5/8, 5/18; 6/13, 6/14
Philippians, letter to 5/14; 6/14
Philistine, Philistines 2/1, 2/2, 2/9, 2/13, 2/14, 2/15; 3/2, 3/9; 7/19; 9/19
philosopher 5/1, 5/8
Phoebe 5/16
Phoenicia, Phoenicians 1/12; 2/18; 9/13
Phrygia 5/2
phylactery 9/20
picnic 8/16
pilgrim, pilgrims 5/2; 7/4, 7/9; 10/2
pirate 9/13
Pisidia 5/6
pitch 1/4
pitcher 10/2
Pithom 1/14
plague 1/16
plains 7/4, 7/17
plaster 8/4, 8/12
Plato 10/9
play 6/17
plough 2/6
ploughing 8/6
plumb-line 9/10, 9/18
poet 2/16
poetry 6/1, 6/7, 6/12, 6/19; 10/5
pollution 1/2, 1/3, 1/5
pomegranate, pomegranates 7/5; 8/6; 9/3, 9/11
Pompey 4/1; 5/4
Pontius Pilate 4/18; 7/15; 9/4
Pontus 5/2
poor, poverty 1/18; 2/1, 2/2, 2/6, 2/11; 3/1, 3/7, 3/9, 3/12; 4/7, 4/8, 4/11, 4/18; 5/17; 6/4, 6/6, 6/13, 6/17, 6/19, 6/20; 8/4, 8/10, 8/19; 9/2, 9/4, 9/5, 9/15; 10/6, 10/7
popcorn 8/15
Porcius Festus 5/13
port 5/5, 5/12
pot 8/15
Potiphar 1/13; 9/7
potsherd 9/16
potter 9/16
pottery 2/3, 2/9; 6/3, 6/9; 8/5; 10/2, 10/4
power 1/13, 1/15; 2/1, 2/3, 2/4; 3/1, 3/8, 3/10, 3/11; 4/1, 4/9, 4/11; 10/6, 10/10, 10/14
powers and principalities 10/10
praise 5/3; 10/13
prayer, prayers 2/19; 4/11, 4/17; 5/3, 5/6, 5/8; 6/7; 8/8; 10/8, 10/13
prayer shawl 9/11
preacher, preaching 5/6

prefect 4/6
priest 2/12, 2/19; 3/13, 3/17, 3/18, 3/19; 4/1, 4/3, 4/5, 4/10, 4/18, 4/20; 5/16; 8/7, 8/8; 9/2, 9/3, 9/5, 9/10, 9/11, 9/15; 10/12, 10/16
prince 1/15, 1/16
princess 1/15; 3/2
printing 6/18
Priscilla 5/9, 5/16
prison 3/2; 5/1, 5/4, 5/8, 5/11, 5/13, 5/14; 9/4
prisoner 3/12; 5/12, 5/13, 5/14, 5/19
Prochorus 5/3
promise 1/8, 1/13, 1/15
prophecy, prophet 2/12, 2/17; 3/2, 3/3, 3/4, 3/5, 3/7, 3/8, 3/9, 3/12, 3/13, 3/15, 3/17, 3/18, 3/19, 3/20; 4/13, 4/16; 5/2, 5/6, 5/12; 6/1, 6/6, 6/9, 6/10, 6/12; 9/10; 10/8, 10/17, 10/19
proselytes 5/5
prostitute 1/18; 2/4
Protestant 6/11
proverbs, Proverbs, book of 2/20; 6/8; 8/10
psalms, Psalms, book of 2/16; 6/7; 8/8; 9/3; 10/7, 10/13
Ptah 1/12
Ptolemais 5/8
Ptolemy II, Philadelphus 6/10
punishment 9/4
purification 8/11
Purim 3/16; 8/7
purse 8/18
pyramid, pyramids 1/1, 1/12; 6/3; 10/1, 10/19

Q

Qarqar 3/6
quarry 3/6; 5/19; 9/18
queen 3/4, 3/6, 3/11
Queen of Sheba 8/13
questions 1/1, 1/2, 1/6
Qumran 7/13; 10/4
Qur'an 7/1

R

rabbi 4/1, 4/7, 4/8, 4/15; 5/3; 8/10, 8/12; 9/11
Rachel 1/10, 1/11
Rahab 2/4, 2/5
rain 3/2, 3/3
rainbow 1/5, 1/6
rainfall 7/5, 7/14, 7/18
raisins 8/4, 8/16
Raameses 7/3
Rameses (city) 1/14
Rameses II 1/14; 2/1
Ramoth-gilead 3/4
ramp 9/9
rats 9/5
rattle 8/13
raven 1/4
Re 1/12
Rebekah 1/9, 1/11
reeds 1/15
Reformation 6/18
Rehoboam 3/1

religion 3/5, 3/7, 3/8
religion, Canaanite 2/3, 2/4
religion, Greek 4/1
religion, Philistine 2/9
religion, Roman 4/2
religious leaders (Jewish) 5/3, 5/6, 5/18
resurrection 4/19; 5/2, 5/20; 8/20; 10/15, 10/19, 10/20
Reuben 1/11; 2/6
Reuben, tribe 7/17
revelation 6/19
Revelation, book of 5/19; 6/14; 10/12, 10/20
rhyme 6/7
rich, riches 8/3, 8/5, 8/19; 10/6, 10/10, 10/14, 10/17
riddle 8/13
riot 5/9
rituals, Canaanite 2/3
rivers 7/1, 7/2, 7/3, 7/4, 7/8, 7/12
road, roads 3/16; 4/2; 5/1, 5/4; 9/12
rock hyrax 7/6
Rome, Romans, Roman Empire 1/12; 3/20; 4/1, 4/2, 4/3, 4/4, 4/5, 4/6, 4/7, 4/8, 4/13, 4/16, 4/19, 4/20; 5/1, 5/2, 5/4, 5/5, 5/6, 5/8, 5/9, 5/12, 5/13, 5/14, 5/15, 5/16, 5/18, 5/20; 6/1, 6/2, 6/12, 6/13, 6/14, 6/16, 6/17; 7/9, 7/13, 7/18, 7/20; 8/3, 8/5, 8/8, 8/13, 8/18, 8/19; 9/1, 9/2, 9/4, 9/6, 9/11, 9/12, 9/15; 10/1, 10/2, 10/4, 10/14, 10/15
Romans, letter to 5/12; 6/14, 6/20
roof 5/5; 8/4
Rosetta stone 10/3
route 1/11
Ruth 2/11; 6/5

S

sabbath 3/14; 4/3, 4/6, 4/19; 5/8, 5/10; 8/13; 9/11
sacrifice 3/3, 3/8, 3/9, 3/14; 8/7, 8/11, 8/15; 9/3; 10/16
Sadducee, Sadducees 4/1; 10/19
Safe harbours 5/13
Salamis 5/6
salt 7/13
salvation history 6/2, 6/13, 6/14
Samaria 3/2, 3/6, 3/7, 3/8; 4/8, 4/10; 5/1; 6/6; 7/2, 7/14
Samaritan 3/17; 4/10
Samson 2/9, 2/10, 2/12; 8/13; 9/6
Samuel 2/10, 2/12, 2/13, 2/16; 9/6; 10/13, 10/19
Samuel, Books of (1 and 2) 6/5
sandal, sandals 3/6; 8/8, 8/18; 9/20; 10/2
Sanhedrin 4/1, 4/16; 9/4
Sarah 1/7, 1/8, 1/9
Sardis 6/14
Saudi Arabia 7/1
Saul (King) 2/1, 2/13, 2/14, 2/15, 2/16, 2/17, 2/18; 7/6; 9/6, 9/8
Saul (follower of Jesus) see Paul
Saviour 4/4
scales 9/10

scapegoat 8/7

school 2/20; 4/6; 8/12; 9/11

science 1/2

scourge 4/18

scribe, scribes 4/1; 6/3; 9/7, 9/11; 10/4

scripture, scriptures 3/7, 3/8, 3/14; 4/1, 4/3;
5/2, 5/4, 5/5, 5/6, 5/7, 5/8, 5/12, 5/13, 5/20;
6/1, 6/10, 6/13, 6/14, 6/15, 6/18; 8/12; 10/16

scroll 6/3, 6/4, 6/9, 6/10, 6/11; 9/11, 9/20; 10/4

sculpture 3/6

Sea peoples see Philistines

seal 9/7

seasons 7/5; 8/6

Sebaste see Samaria

secretary 5/11; 9/7

seed 10/19

Sekhmet 1/12

Seleucia 5/6

Sennacherib 3/9; 10/3

Sepphoris 7/9; 9/18

Septuagint 6/10, 6/11, 6/15; 10/17

Sergius Paulus 5/6

servant 3/5; 8/1, 8/9, 8/16

Sethos 2/1

settlers 2/6; 9/1

Shadrach 3/14

Shalmaneser III 3/6

Shalmaneser V 3/8

Shamgar 2/9

share, sharing 2/6

Sheba, Queen of 2/18, 2/20

Shechem 2/6; 3/1; 9/9

sheep 3/13, 3/20; 6/12; 7/6, 7/10, 7/14; 8/2,
8/12, 8/17

shellfish 8/15

Shelters, festival of 6/9

Shema 9/7

Sheol 8/19; 10/19

shepherd, shepherds 1/3, 1/16; 2/15, 2/16;
3/7, 3/13; 4/4, 4/13; 6/12, 6/17; 7/10; 9/10

Sheshbazzar 3/17

shield 9/8, 9/9, 9/20

Shiloh 2/10, 2/12, 2/13

ship 2/9, 2/18; 5/6, 5/13; 9/13

shofar 1/20

showbread 4/3

shrine 2/3

Sicily 5/13

sick people 3/13; 10/2

Sidon 9/13

siege 3/6, 3/9, 3/12; 9/9

sieve 3/7

Silas 5/8, 5/16

silver 1/17, 1/18; 3/5; 5/9; 6/8; 9/19

Simeon 1/11; 2/6

Simon (follower of Jesus) see Peter

Simon (the leatherworker) 5/5

sin 8/7; 10/10, 10/16

Sinai, Mount 1/17, 1/19; 2/1; 3/4; 6/3; 7/1, 7/3;
10/4

Sinaiticus, Codex 10/4

singing 8/8, 8/9

Sisera 2/7

sister 8/1, 8/19

slave, slaves, slavery 1/6, 1/11, 1/13, 1/14,
1/15, 1/16, 1/17, 1/19; 2/1, 2/2, 2/4, 2/6, 2/11,
2/13, 2/19, 2/20; 3/1, 3/2; 5/6, 5/8, 5/10, 5/14;
6/4, 6/5, 6/15; 8/8; 9/1, 9/2, 9/5; 10/17, 10/20

Slavonic, Old 6/16

slinger 3/6

slingshot 2/15; 8/13

Smyrna 6/14

snake 1/3

snow 7/5

soap 8/19

Sobek 1/12

Sodom 7/13

soldier, soldiers 2/6, 2/13, 2/14, 2/17, 2/19;
3/8; 4/2, 4/5, 4/17, 4/18; 5/5, 5/8, 5/12, 5/14;
10/14, 10/17

Solomon 2/1, 2/18, 2/19, 2/20; 3/1, 3/7, 3/8;
6/5; 7/7, 7/8, 7/14, 7/15; 9/2, 9/4, 9/6, 9/7,
9/8, 9/9, 9/13; 10/8, 10/16

Son of God 5/2, 5/3

song 2/20; 6/5, 6/7

Song of Solomon 2/20; 6/7

soul 10/19

sowing 2/6; 8/6

Spain 3/19; 5/14

spear 9/8

spices 2/18; 8/16

spindle 8/17

spinning 8/17

spirit 10/16, 10/17, 10/18

Spirit see Holy Spirit

spring 7/5

spy 2/2, 2/4, 2/5

St Catherine's monastery 6/3; 10/4

St Paul's Bay (Malta) 5/13

stained glass 6/17

star 4/5

Stephanus, Robert 6/18

Stephen 5/3, 5/4, 5/5, 5/16

stew 8/15, 8/16

steward 1/9; 9/7

stone 1/12; 4/6; 8/5; 9/18

stoning 3/4; 5/3

story 6/2, 6/4, 6/5, 6/12, 6/19

storytelling 8/13; 10/5

stove 8/14

string 9/4

stucco 8/5

suffering 4/12, 4/13, 4/18, 4/19; 5/11, 5/19

suicide 5/2

Sumer, Sumerian, Sumerians 1/1, 1/5; 3/11;
7/2

summer 7/5; 8/4

Sunday 5/10

supernatural 10/1

Susa 3/6, 3/11, 3/16; 7/2

swaddling 8/11

sword 9/8

symbol 10/8, 10/10

synagogue 3/14; 4/6; 5/2, 5/4, 5/5, 5/6, 5/8;
6/4, 6/10; 7/9; 8/7, 8/10, 8/12, 8/19; 9/11;
10/2, 10/16

synoptic Gospels 6/13

Syria, Syrians 2/9; 3/3, 3/5, 3/6, 3/8; 4/1; 5/4,
5/6, 5/8, 5/13; 6/16; 7/1, 7/7, 7/18; 9/8; 10/1,
10/11

Syriac 6/16

T

tabernacle 1/18; 8/7; 9/2, 9/3; 10/16

Tabernacles, festival 1/20; 8/7

tablet (clay stone) 3/6; 10/5, 10/8

Tabor, Mount 2/7

tambourine 6/7; 8/13; 9/3

tanner 9/20

tar 1/6, 1/15

Targum 6/9

Tarsus 5/4, 5/13; 7/18

tassel 8/18

tax 10/8

tax collector 4/1; 9/15; 10/15

taxes 2/14, 2/18, 2/19; 3/1, 3/16; 4/4, 4/16;
5/15; 9/6, 9/7, 9/15

teacher 4/1, 4/5, 4/7, 4/8, 4/10, 4/14, 4/15;
5/18

Tekoa 3/7

Tel Aviv 7/7

tell (mound) 10/1

temple 1/18, 1/20; 2/10, 2/12, 2/19, 2/20; 3/1,
3/9, 3/10, 3/12, 3/13, 3/14, 3/17, 3/18, 3/19;
4/3, 4/5, 4/6, 4/7, 4/16; 5/2, 5/3, 5/8, 5/11,
5/12, 5/20; 6/4, 6/7, 6/8, 6/11; 7/1, 7/7, 7/15;
8/7, 8/8, 8/10, 8/12, 8/19; 9/2, 9/3, 9/10, 9/11;
10/1, 10/16, 10/18

Ten Commandments 1/19, 1/20; 6/4; 9/2

tent 1/7, 1/18, 1/20; 8/2, 8/16

tentmaking 5/6, 5/8, 5/16

tephillin 9/20
testament 1/20
Testaments (Old and New) 6/1–6/20; 10/4
thanksgiving 10/13
theatre *see* amphitheatre
Thessalonians, letter to 5/16, 5/19; 6/14
Thessalonica 5/8, 5/16, 5/19; 6/14
Thomas 4/19
threshing 8/6, 8/12
throne 10/3
thummin 10/12
Thyatira 5/8; 6/14
Tiamat 10/5
Tiberias 7/9
Tiglath-Pileser 2/1; 3/6
Tiglath-Pileser III 3/8
Tigris, River 6/3; 7/2, 7/6
Timnath-serah 2/6
Timon 5/3
Timothy 5/8, 5/16; 6/1
Timothy, letters to 5/17; 6/14
Tischendorf, Constantin von 10/4
tithe 9/15
Titus 5/16; 6/14
Titus, letter to 5/17
Titus (Emperor) 5/16
tomb 4/18, 4/19; 8/19; 10/15
tongues, speaking in 5/10
tools 9/17, 9/18
Torah 6/4

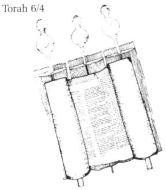

torch 2/8
tower 1/6
Tower of Babel 1/6
town 8/1
toy 8/13
trade, traders 2/3; 4/3; 8/10, 8/12; 9/12, 9/13, 9/14
Trans-Jordan region 7/17
translation 6/1, 6/9, 6/10, 6/11, 6/16, 6/18
travel 4/2
travelling 7/4, 7/6, 7/13
treason 3/4
treasure 9/19
trial 5/3, 5/13
tribe 8/1
tribes 2/6, 2/12
tribes (of Israel) 3/8
Trinity 10/18
Troas 5/8
Trophimus 5/12
trumpet 9/3

trumpets 2/5, 2/8
Trumpets, festival of 1/20; 8/7
truth 6/19
tunic 8/18
Turkey 5/4, 5/6, 5/14
Turkey *see* Asia Minor
Tychicus 6/14
Tyrannus 5/9
Tyre 2/18, 2/19; 3/2; 5/8; 9/13

U

Ugarit 2/1, 2/3
uncle 8/1
unleavened bread 8/8
Ur 1/7; 8/2; 9/19
Uriah 2/17
urim 10/12

V

valleys 7/4, 7/5, 7/8, 7/12
vegetables 8/6, 8/16
veil 8/9
vellum 6/3
verse 6/18
villa 5/10
village 8/1
vine 4/13; 8/6
vineyard 3/4, 3/7; 8/10
violence 4/18; 8/1; 10/5
viper 7/6
virgin 10/14
vision 3/2; 5/4; 10/12
visitor 8/2
Vulgate 6/16, 6/18

W

wall, walls 3/17, 3/18; 8/3, 8/12
war 1/3, 1/12; 6/5; 7/2, 7/8, 7/15, 7/18; 9/8, 9/9, 9/12, 9/13
warrior 2/15, 2/16, 2/17, *see also* battle
washing 8/16, 8/19
water 4/14; 8/2, 8/3, 8/4, 8/16
water supply 3/9
wealth 3/1, 3/7, 3/8, 3/15; 5/17; 6/8; 9/15
weapons 4/5
weaving 8/17
wedding 8/9, 8/13, 8/18
Weeks, festival of *see* Pentecost
weights and measures 9/14
well 8/2
wheat 8/6, 8/15
wheel 9/12, 9/16
whipping 9/4
whistle 8/13
widow 8/9; 10/6
wife 3/7, 3/8, 3/19; 8/1, 8/9
wind 5/2; 10/17
wine 4/17; 5/10; 8/5, 8/6, 8/8, 8/14, 8/16; 9/7; 10/16
wineskin 9/20

winnowing 8/6
winter 7/5
wisdom 2/20; 6/8, 6/10
wise men 4/5
wolf 7/12
women 8/1, 8/10
wood 1/12; 4/6; 9/8, 9/17
wool 8/2, 8/10, 8/17
workshop 8/3
worship 1/16, 1/18; 2/3, 2/6, 2/17; 3/1, 3/3, 3/4, 3/5, 3/7, 3/9, 3/10, 3/13, 3/14, 3/18, 3/19; 4/2; 5/10, 5/15; 6/4, 6/5, 6/7, 6/11, 6/15; 8/13; 9/2, 9/3; 10/8, 10/16
writing 2/3; 6/3; 9/7; 10/3, 10/4
wrongdoer, wrongdoing 1/4, 1/6, 1/19; 10/6, 10/10, 10/15, 10/16, *see also* sin

Y

Yadin, Yigael 10/1
Yahweh 1/16
Yarmuq, River 7/17
yeast 8/8, 8/15
Yehudi 9/10
yoghurt 8/15

Z

Zealots 4/1
Zebulun 1/11; 2/6
Zechariah 3/17, 3/20; 4/3, 4/7; 6/6; 10/9
Zedekiah 3/12
Zephaniah 6/6
Zerubbabel 3/17, 3/20
Zeus 3/20
ziggurat 1/6

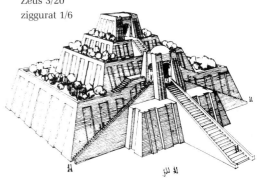

Zilpah 1/11
Zion 3/12, 3/15; 4/3
Zion, Mount 6/11

Old Testament at a glance

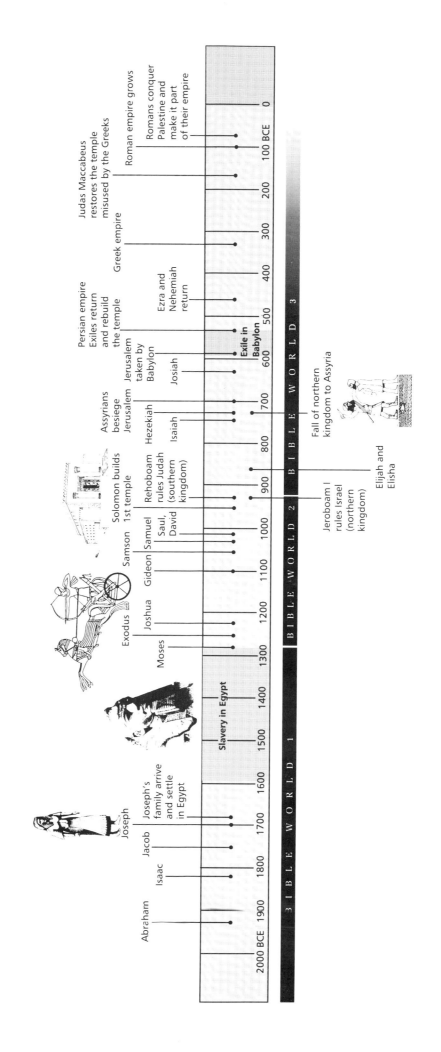

Abraham

Isaac

Jacob

Joseph

Joseph's family arrive and settle in Egypt

Slavery in Egypt

Moses

Exodus

Joshua

Gideon

Samson

Samuel

Saul, David

Solomon builds 1st temple

Rehoboam rules Judah (southern kingdom)

Jeroboam I rules Israel (northern kingdom)

Elijah and Elisha

Fall of northern kingdom to Assyria

Assyrians besiege Jerusalem

Hezekiah

Isaiah

Jerusalem taken by Babylon

Josiah

Exile in Babylon

Persian empire
Exiles return and rebuild the temple

Ezra and Nehemiah return

Greek empire

Judas Maccabeus restores the temple misused by the Greeks

Roman empire grows

Romans conquer Palestine and make it part of their empire

2000 BCE 1900 1800 1700 1600 1500 1400 1300 1200 1100 1000 900 800 700 600 500 400 300 200 100 BCE 0

BIBLE WORLD 1   BIBLE WORLD 2   BIBLE WORLD 3

New Testament at a glance

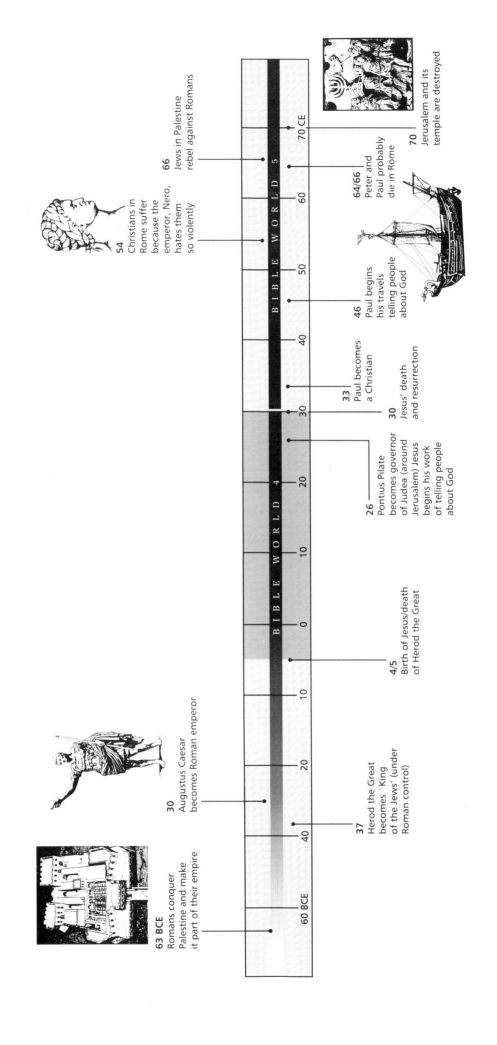

63 BCE
Romans conquer Palestine and make it part of their empire

60 BCE

37
Herod the Great becomes 'King of the Jews' (under Roman control)

40

30
Augustus Caesar becomes Roman emperor

20

10

BIBLE WORLD 4

0

4/5
Birth of Jesus/death of Herod the Great

10

20

26
Pontius Pilate becomes governor of Judea (around Jerusalem) Jesus begins his work of telling people about God

30

30
Jesus' death and resurrection

33
Paul becomes a Christian

40

BIBLE WORLD 5

46
Paul begins his travels telling people about God

50

54
Christians in Rome suffer because the emperor, Nero, hates them so violently

60

64/66
Peter and Paul probably die in Rome

66
Jews in Palestine rebel against Romans

70 CE

70
Jerusalem and its temple are destroyed